Granville County Library System
P.O. Box 339
Oxford, NC 27565

DISCARD

P9-CLP-392

REMARKABLE PEOPLE

Steve Jobs

by Steve Goldsworthy

AV2
MEDIA ENHANCED BOOKS
BY WEIGL
ADDED VALUE • AUDIO VISUAL

www.av2books.com

AV² provides enriched content that supplements and complements this book. Weigl's AV² books strive to create inspired learning and engage young minds in a total learning experience.

Your AV² Media Enhanced books come alive with...

Audio
Listen to sections of the book read aloud.

Key Words
Study vocabulary, and complete a matching word activity.

Video
Watch informative video clips.

Quizzes
Test your knowledge.

Go to www.av2books.com, and enter this book's unique code.

Embedded Weblinks
Gain additional information for research.

Slide Show
View images and captions, and prepare a presentation.

BOOK CODE

N 2 6 6 1 8 9

Try This!
Complete activities and hands-on experiments.

... and much, much more!

AV² by Weigl brings you media enhanced books that support active learning.

Published by AV² by Weigl
350 5th Avenue, 59th Floor
New York, NY 10118

www.av2books.com   www.weigl.com

Copyright ©2012 AV² by Weigl

All rights reserved. No part of this publication may be reproduced, stored in a retrieval system, or transmitted in any form or by any means, electronic, mechanical, photocopying, recording, or otherwise, without the prior written permission of the publisher.

Library of Congress Cataloging-in-Publication Data

Goldsworthy, Steve.
  Steve Jobs / Steve Goldsworthy.
    p. cm. -- (Remarkable people)
  Includes index.
  ISBN 978-1-61690-670-2 (hardcover : alk. paper) -- ISBN 978-1-61690-675-7 (softcover : alk. paper)
  1. Jobs, Steven, 1955- 2. Businesspeople--Biography--Juvenile literature. 3. Computer engineers--United States--Biography--Juvenile literature. 4. Computer industry--United States--Juvenile literature. 5. Apple Computer, Inc.--Juvenile literature. I. Title.
  HD9696.2.U62J6355 2011
  338.761004'092--dc22
                          2010050999

Printed in the United States of American in North Mankato, Minnesota
1 2 3 4 5 6 7 8 9 0 15 14 13 12 11

WEP37500
052011

Editor: Heather Kissock
Art Director: Terry Paulhus

Photograph Credits
Weigl acknowledges Getty Images as the primary image supplier for this title.

Every reasonable effort has been made to trace ownership and to obtain permission to reprint copyright material. The publishers would be pleased to have any errors or omissions brought to their attention so that they may be corrected in subsequent printings.

Contents

Who Is Steve Jobs?

Steve Jobs is one of the best-known people in the computer industry. He is the co-founder and **chief executive officer (CEO)** of one of the most successful companies of all time, Apple Inc. Apple is responsible for the development of the computer known as the Macintosh, or Mac. The company has also created the iPod, the iPhone and more recently, the iPad. As an inventor, Steve holds more than 230 patents, or exclusive rights, to equipment such as computers, portable devices, keyboards, and computer mouses.

"We started out to get a computer in the hands of everyday people, and we succeeded beyond our wildest dreams."

Steve Jobs was also the CEO of Pixar Animation Studios, the movie company that has produced such hits as *Toy Story*, *The Incredibles*, and *UP*. He now sits on the **board of directors** at Walt Disney Studios. Here, he provides direction and offers advice on projects the studio is planning.

Growing Up

Steven Paul Jobs was born in San Francisco, California, on February 24, 1955. Shortly after his birth, he was **adopted** by Paul and Clara Jobs. They raised Steve in the city of Cupertino. The city is in a part of California known as Silicon Valley. The valley is known as the birthplace of many of the world's leading technology companies. Several computer-industry companies, such as Google, the Internet search-engine company, have their main offices there.

Growing up, Steve was an average student. This changed when his family moved to the city of Los Altos. Many of his new neighbors were working in the exciting new field of electronics. Steve began talking to them about their work. Soon, he was using home electronics kits to make various devices.

In high school, Steve met another student named Stephen Wozniak. Stephen was known as Woz to his friends. Woz was building a **circuit board** and was impressed that Steve understood how it worked. Soon, the two boys were working together on various electronics projects. Over time, Steve's fascination with electronics led him to a job at Atari, one of the first video-game companies.

■ Stephen Wozniak invited Steve to become a member of the Homebrew Computer Club, a group he belonged to. Here, Steve and Wozniak began making homemade computers.

Get to Know California

BIRD
California
Valley Quail

FLAG

ANIMAL
California
Grizzly Bear

California is the most heavily populated state in America, with more than 33 million people.

Death Valley is considered the hottest spot in North America. On July 10, 1913, the hottest temperature in the Western Hemisphere was recorded there, at 134 °F (57 °C).

With more than 3.8 million people, Los Angeles, California, is the second most populated city in the United States, behind New York City.

From 1967 to 1975, California's governor was former actor Ronald Reagan. He went on to become the 40th president of the United States.

Think about it!

Silicon Valley is considered by many to be the center of technological **innovation**. Companies such as Hewlett-Packard and Intel Corporation have developed computer technologies that make many basic tasks easier. How have computers changed your life? Do you work with computers at school or at home? Can you think of any ideas that could improve the way people and computers work together?

Practice Makes Perfect

In the early 1970s, computing was still a new science. There were companies using computers, but these machines took up entire rooms and were very complicated to run. Steve Jobs had a vision. He saw a future where regular, everyday people would have their own computers. They could work on computers in their offices and use them at home. They could even take their computers with them. These computers would help make people's lives easier.

Other people had similar ideas and were working toward making computers smaller and easier to use. Computer technology changed in 1974 when Intel Corporation introduced the 8080 **microprocessor.** This was the first microprocessor to be affordable and powerful enough to be used in a personal computer.

■ Intel developed the 4004 microprocessor in 1971. The technology used in the 4004 eventually led to the creation of the 8080.

This technology helped Stephen Wozniak create a new type of personal computer. This computer was the first to directly connect the keyboard and screen to the computer itself. In earlier versions, users had to access the computer remotely through a terminal.

QUICK FACTS

- Steve and Wozniak built their first Apple computers in the Jobs family's garage.

- Steve sold his Volkswagen car to get money to start his company.

- Steve receives about 300 emails every day.

When Steve saw what his friend had done, he knew instantly that this was the technology his ideas had been waiting for. He set to work with Woz, building and selling the computers. Recalling an earlier job he once had at an apple orchard, Steve came up with the name Apple for the company.

■ The Apple I, Apple's first computer, went on sale in July 1976 at a price of $666.66.

Key Events

In 1977, Steve and his company developed the Apple II, the first color computer. It had **high-resolution graphics** and sound.

It was at about this time that Steve met businessman Mike Markkula. Mike joined the company with the aim of taking Apple to the top of the computer world. He started a **marketing campaign** to advertise the Apple II. He hired people to create a company **logo** and design a case for the Apple II. As a result of his marketing efforts, the Apple II began to sell very well. Apple went from selling 2,500 computers in 1977 to more than 35,000 in 1979. Steve became a multimillionaire in only two years.

In 1986, Steve acquired the computer graphics division of another company. He named his new company Pixar. The company used computers to make animated films. Their work caught the attention of Disney Studios. The two companies worked together to produce the movie *Toy Story* in 1995. In the following years, Pixar went on produce *Finding Nemo*, *Cars*, and *WALL-E*.

■ The creation of the Apple II is considered the start of the personal computer craze.

Thoughts from Steve

Steve Jobs has worked hard to achieve his success and has experienced many challenges along the way. Here are some of his comments about his beliefs regarding work and life.

Steve and Apple put great emphasis on the design of their products.

"Design is not just what it looks like and feels like. Design is how it works."

Steve knows the value of quality.

"Be a yardstick of quality. Some people aren't used to an environment where excellence is expected."

Steve realizes everyone makes mistakes.

"...Sometimes when you innovate, you make mistakes. It is best to admit them quickly, and get on with improving your other innovations."

To be successful, Steve believes you must always strive to do things in a new and better way.

"Innovation distinguishes a leader from a follower."

Steve talks about staying a step ahead.

"You can't just ask customers what they want and then try to give that to them. By the time you get it built, they'll want something new."

Steve talks about what it takes to be successful.

"I'm convinced that about half of what separates the successful **entrepreneurs** from the non-successful ones is pure perseverance."

What Is a Computer Innovator?

An innovator is a person who introduces new methods or procedures that change the way things are done. Being an innovator means being able to think creatively. Innovators are not afraid to try something, even if others think it will not work.

The world of computers is filled with innovators. Many computer innovators are scientists with training in engineering, electronics, chemistry, or physics. Some computer innovators are untrained amateurs who are fascinated with computers and the way they work.

There have been many inventors who have contributed to the creation of computers today. However, there is no one person who is solely responsible for their invention. Instead, people have continued to experiment and build upon ideas and technologies that have gone before them. The use of the abacus in ancient times shows that people have been thinking about using machines to do calculations for thousands of years.

■ An abacus is a calculating tool that can be used to solve arithmetic problems.

Computer Innovators 101

Bill Hewlett (1913–2001) and David Packard (1912–1996)

In 1939, Bill Hewlett and David Packard started the electronics company Hewlett-Packard (HP) in Packard's garage in Palo Alto, California. The company is recognized as establishing the area known as Silicon Valley. Today, HP is the biggest computer company in the world, making more than $114 billion in sales in 2009.

Konrad Zuse (1910–1995)

Konrad Zuse was a German **engineer** who developed the first programmable computer, the Z3, in 1941. The program that ran the computer was on a long paper tape punched with holes. Zuse could change the function of the computer by changing the holes in the tape, something that had never been seen before. These computers were used to design missiles and other weapons in World War II.

Henry Edward Roberts (1941– 2010)

Ed Roberts is considered by the industry as the father of the personal computer. In 1969, Ed founded Micro Instrumentation and Telemetry Systems (MITS). He designed and helped construct the first commercially available personal computer, the Altair 8800, in 1975. Roberts later sold MITS and became a doctor.

Bill Gates (1955–)

Bill Gates is the cofounder of one of the biggest computer companies in the world, Microsoft Corporation. In 1975, Bill and Paul Allen, a childhood friend, began making software for an Altair microprocessor. Today, Gates is considered one of the wealthiest people in the world. He gives billions of dollars to charity through his Bill and Melinda Gates Foundation.

Apple versus Microsoft

Two of the biggest computer rivals in the world are Apple Inc. and Microsoft Corporation. The companies have two very different approaches to computers and their market. Microsoft gained a big foothold in the corporate world, while Apple focused on artistic workers such as designers and graphic artists. Microsoft has traditionally held a bigger share of the computer market, but Apple, with its focus on devices like the iPod and iTouch, has now begun to surpass Microsoft.

Influences

Steve credits his teachers as influences in his life. One teacher who took early note of Steve's interest in technology was Mr. McCollum. He taught high-school electronics. Under Mr. McCollum's guidance, Steve was soon building different types of electronic devices.

One week, Mr. McCollum gave Steve a homework project. To complete the project, Steve needed spare parts. He called a local company to see if it had what he needed. That local company was Hewlett-Packard. Steve ended up speaking to Bill Hewlett himself. Mr. McCollum was shocked, especially when he learned that Steve had been given a summer job out of the meeting.

■ Hewlett-Packard's headquarters is located in Palo Alto, California.

Steve gained knowledge and inspiration from his time as a member of the Homebrew Computer Club. The group met at California's Stanford University and discussed personal computers and electronics. Steve spent hours exchanging ideas and tips on constructing do-it-yourself computer kits. The knowledge he gained from the other members inspired him to build Apple years later.

THE JOBS FAMILY

Steve married Laurene Powell, a business student at Stanford University, on March 18, 1991. Together, they have three children, a son, Reed Paul, and two daughters, Erin and Eve. Steve has another daughter, Lisa, from a previous relationship.

■ Steve met Laurene when he was a guest speaker at Stanford University.

Overcoming Obstacles

Competition is an important part of any business. Companies are constantly developing better products and services to outdo their rivals. This usually leads to great benefits for the customers.

When starting out, Steve Jobs and Apple had to deal with competition from big companies. In 1976, Steve was at the Personal Computer Festival in Atlantic City trying to sell his Apple I computer. His stand was next to one from a much larger company. It had salespeople in business suits, music, and even dancers. Steve looked like an amateur next to them. He did not get upset, however. Instead, Steve used the situation to learn about the value of promotion and marketing. He went home and began taking steps to make Apple a more **professional** company.

■ When attending technology conferences, Apple Inc. uses large booths and attractive signage to advertise its products.

Despite Apple's success, Steve disagreed with the company's board of directors on how the company should be run. In 1985, he agreed to step down as chairman of the board and leave the company. It was a tough time for Steve, but his creative spirit was never crushed. He bought Pixar and formed another computer company, called NeXT, as well. In 1996, Apple bought NeXT, and Steve returned to his former company. He became its chief executive officer the following year.

In 2004, Steve was diagnosed with pancreatic cancer. He had the cancerous tumor removed, but his health remained a problem. In 2009, he had to return to the hospital for a liver transplant. Even though he had to take time away from work for treatment, he returned to the company and continued to promote its products.

■ When the iPad was introduced in 2010, Steve used his Pixar connection to advertise the new Apple technology.

Achievements and Successes

Steve Jobs has continued to create and develop new computer technologies. In 2001, Steve and his team at Apple introduced the iPod, a portable music device. The iPod is used to store or play music files that have been **downloaded** from the Internet.

Apple introduced the iPhone in 2007. This **multi-touch** telephone allows people to make phone calls, listen to music, surf the Internet, and even watch movies. The iPod Touch was introduced at the same time, doing everything the iPhone did, but without the phone service.

In 2010, Apple launched the iPad, a much larger version of the iTouch. The iPad offers a range of **applications** that allow the user to do everything from play games and read books to navigate the globe with Google maps.

■ Steve traveled to London in 2007 to introduce the iPhone to the British people. The iPhone is now available in more than 40 countries.

Steve's innovative thinking has been rewarded in many ways. In 2007, he was inducted into the California Hall of Fame. That same year, *Fortune Magazine* named him the most powerful person in the world of business. In 2009 and 2010, the Junior Achievement Organization voted Steve the most admired entrepreneur.

HELPING THE ENVIRONMENT

Apple Inc. is committed to protecting the global environment. The company constantly monitors its manufacturing processes to make sure it limits the amount of **greenhouse gases** created. Apple also makes special efforts to produce technologies that are energy efficient. In fact, some of its computers use less energy than a standard light bulb. Many of the materials used to make an Apple computer are recyclable. Apple will help customers find recycling companies to dispose of their old computers. This also helps Apple limit its impact on the environment.

Write a Biography

A person's life story can be the subject of a book. This kind of book is called a biography. Biographies describe the lives of remarkable people, such as those who have achieved great success or have done important things to help others. These people may be alive today, or they may have lived many years ago. Reading a biography can help you learn more about a remarkable person.

At school, you might be asked to write a biography. First, decide who you want to write about. You can choose a computer innovator, such as Steve Jobs, or any other person. Then, find out if your library has any books about this person. Learn as much as you can about him or her. Write down the key events in this person's life. What was this person's childhood like? What has he or she accomplished? What are his or her goals? What makes this person special or unusual?

A concept web is a useful research tool. Read the questions in the following concept web. Answer the questions in your notebook. Your answers will help you write a biography.

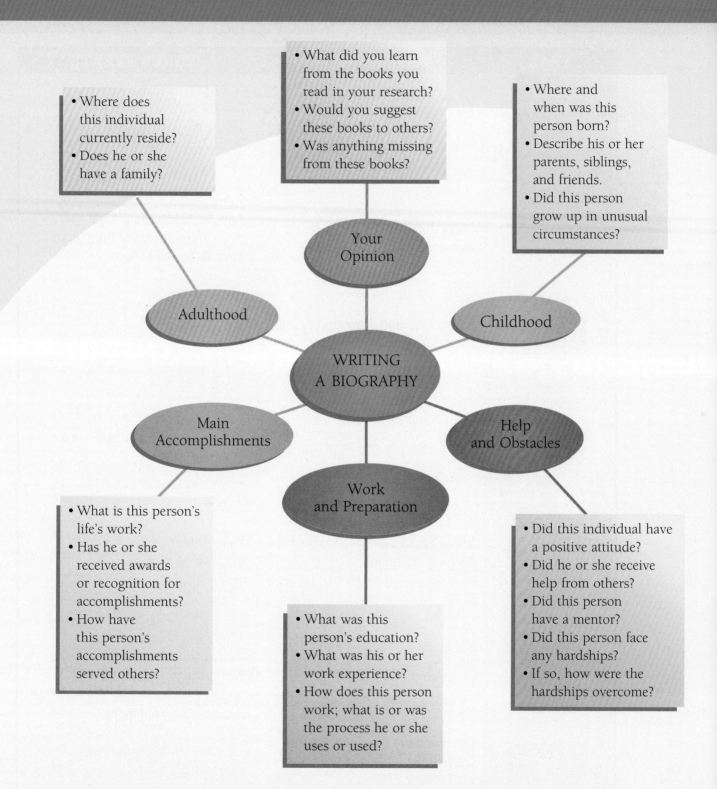

- Where does this individual currently reside?
- Does he or she have a family?

- What did you learn from the books you read in your research?
- Would you suggest these books to others?
- Was anything missing from these books?

- Where and when was this person born?
- Describe his or her parents, siblings, and friends.
- Did this person grow up in unusual circumstances?

Your Opinion

Adulthood

Childhood

WRITING A BIOGRAPHY

Main Accomplishments

Help and Obstacles

Work and Preparation

- What is this person's life's work?
- Has he or she received awards or recognition for accomplishments?
- How have this person's accomplishments served others?

- What was this person's education?
- What was his or her work experience?
- How does this person work; what is or was the process he or she uses or used?

- Did this individual have a positive attitude?
- Did he or she receive help from others?
- Did this person have a mentor?
- Did this person face any hardships?
- If so, how were the hardships overcome?

Timeline

YEAR	STEVE JOBS	WORLD EVENTS
1955	Steven Paul Jobs is born on February 24.	Albert Einstein dies on April 18.
1969	Steve Jobs meets future Apple cofounder Stephen Wozniak.	American astronaut Neil Armstrong becomes first person to walk on the Moon.
1976	Steve Jobs and Stephen Wozniak launch Apple Computer Inc. on April 1.	Bill Gates and Paul Allen register Microsoft as their company name.
1985	Steve Jobs resigns from Apple.	The first Internet **domain name** is registered.
1986	Steve buys Pixar Animation Studios.	Fuji introduces the disposable camera.
1997	Steve Jobs becomes chief executive officer of Apple again.	IBM's Deep Blue computer defeats chess champion Garry Kasparov for the first time.
2010	Following the iPod and iPhone, Steve Jobs introduces the iPad on January 27.	Dr. Kenneth Matsumura invents the artificial liver.

Words to Know

adopted: taken into one's family through legal means and raised as one's own child

applications: computer software designed to help the user perform specific tasks

board of directors: a group of people chosen to govern the affairs of a company

chief executive officer (CEO): the highest ranking manager or administrator in a company

circuit board: the panel on which a computer's components are connected

domain name: a name owned by a person or organization and used as an Internet address

downloaded: saved to a computer, often from the Internet

engineer: a highly skilled technician or scientist who develops ways and devices to make things work

entrepreneurs: people who create and take responsibility for a new company, invention, or idea

greenhouse gases: gases in the atmosphere that trap the Sun's energy and contribute to rising temperatures

high-resolution graphics: images that can be seen vividly and printed clearly

innovation: a new way of thinking or doing something

logo: a symbol used to represent a company

marketing campaign: a series of activities used to advertise a product or service

microprocessor: a chip that contains a circuit of electrical components that can process programs, remember information, and perform calculations

multi-touch: the ability for a touch-screen device to take several touches at once

professional: having businesslike standards and conduct

Index

Log on to www.av2books.com

AV² by Weigl brings you media enhanced books that support active learning. Go to www.av2books.com, and enter the special code found on page 2 of this book. You will gain access to enriched and enhanced content that supplements and complements this book. Content includes video, audio, web links, quizzes, a slide show, and activities.

Audio
Listen to sections of the book read aloud.

Video
Watch informative video clips.

Embedded Weblinks
Gain additional information for research.

Try This!
Complete activities and hands-on experiments.

WHAT'S ONLINE?

Try This!	Embedded Weblinks	Video	EXTRA FEATURES
Complete an activity about your childhood.	Learn more about Steve Jobs' life.	Watch a video about Steve Jobs.	**Audio** Listen to sections of the book read aloud.
Try this activity about key events.	Learn more about Steve Jobs' achievements.	Check out another video about Steve Jobs.	**Key Words** Study vocabulary, and complete a matching word activity.
Complete an activity about overcoming obstacles.	Check out this site about Steve Jobs.		**Slide Show** View images and captions, and prepare a presentation.
Write a biography.			
Try this timeline activity.			**Quizzes** Test your knowledge.

AV² was built to bridge the gap between print and digital. We encourage you to tell us what you like and what you want to see in the future.

Sign up to be an AV² Ambassador at www.av2books.com/ambassador.

Due to the dynamic nature of the Internet, some of the URLs and activities provided as part of AV² by Weigl may have changed or ceased to exist. AV² by Weigl accepts no responsibility for any such changes. All media enhanced books are regularly monitored to update addresses and sites in a timely manner. Contact AV² by Weigl at 1-866-649-3445 or av2books@weigl.com with any questions, comments, or feedback.